"Stories My Mother Never Told Me"

By Diana Lee

&

The Boomerang Book

To Be Written By A Loved One

This book is in memory of my Mom, for all the stories she never told me…

There were none.

1 Corinthians 16:14 ~ Let all that you do be done in love.

"Stories My Mother Never Told Me"

My mom was probably one of the last great story tellers, ever! I swear she had a million of them, some she told over and over and over; even if you tried to stop her and say, "Mom, you already told me that one." Then we'd tease her, telling her she should write a book; in which she would agree…but alas, she never did. And here I sit now, trying to remember just one of her stories <BLANK STARE> I was in a panic…so in an effort to stimulate my memory, I decided to try sending a text message to my brother and sister, since nobody actually talks on the phone anymore, which is probably one of the reasons storytelling is practically a lost art. My text message read: Help! Mom had a million stories, but for the life of me, I can't remember a single one!

Well, it worked! Within minutes, I had received messages from both my brother and sister, with stories of Mom, and from there…my memory banks opened up as well. My sister, who is the youngest, remembered stories about mom helping to sell War Bonds, and that made me remember her story of going to the USO dances in Chicago, to meet up with the soldiers when they would come home on leave. Then my brother, the middle child, recalled the story of her flying in a small airplane which was owned by her boyfriend, and how he flew it sideways, right through these huge arches near The Modernage Furniture store in Miami. Oh yes, she loved to tell that one! In which that story reminded me of what a dare-devil she was and how she would talk about being an acrobatic Roller Skater, and how the guys would spin her around and she would pick up a handkerchief with her teeth, I kid you not! So these are just a few of the milder ones, I will not be writing any of the truly crazy ones here, as those will be left for me to share in "The Boomerang Book" and only for a select few to read…if you catch my drift.

I'm sure you're trying to figure out why I call this "Stories My Mother Never Told Me," right? Well I have a story of my own about that...and it goes like this. One day when I was at work at my Hair Salon, I was sitting up at the desk and had just finished telling my mom something that had recently happened to me, in which she proceeded to say, "Oh that's like the time I..." and you see where I'm going with this. I chuckled and said, "Mom, you told me that story, like a few times!" But she told me again anyway, cause that's how she rolled. And I listened, smiling at her, thinking of what I was going to do next. So after my mom walked away to do her client's manicure; I began to write my very first book! I stapled a bunch of blank pages together, and wrote on the cover, "Stories My Mother Never Told Me," and of course, the inside was blank; because as you have probably figured out by now, she told me every single one of them, and I'm happy she did...if only she had written them down. Because sadly, even though our love for someone never fades; it seems many of our memories, do just that. So back to the story; later that day I showed her the book I'd put together and we laughed about it, because my mom had a great sense of humor and an ability to laugh at herself, and I guess that is why, in spite of her flaws, she was so darn utterly charming.

I began to think of the day we put our mom to rest, and of the eulogy I had written for her, which in part said, "I never knew how much I'd miss her, until I heard the silence," and that just about says it all. Those little gems she shared with us now seem to be locked up tight away, but not for safe keeping I fear...this makes me sad.

I suppose this all has something to do with a road trip I took with my youngest son years later, when he was moving to New York. I ask if I could ride with him and make it a bit of a vacation for myself, as well as keeping him company and then I'd fly back home one way. He agreed, and I told him I was going to bore him silly throughout the journey with little tidbits of my life and that's exactly what I did, feeling much like my own mom the entire time. Some of the stories I am sure he had heard before... like the one where I jumped head first into the shallow end of the pool at sleep away Church Camp, painfully hitting my head on the bottom; lucky to not have been paralyzed, but I believe God was with me. I especially would use this story as a teaching moment for each of my boys when they were heading off to Church Camp themselves, telling them to make sure that

they knew which end was the deep end, before jumping in. And I also told him the story of how my girlfriends and I would cut through the graveyard on our way home from school sometimes, and how one time I picked up the planks covering a future grave, just to look inside. When the caretaker came out of nowhere, yelling "Hey you kids!" and we ran as fast as we could, hearing him saying, "come back here, I'll put you in there!" My son sure cracked up hearing that story.

I believe story's like these humanizes us, and it's really a shame we don't sit around and actually talk anymore, like in the good old days before televisions and cell phones. I think what we could use today is a good fireside chat, but that's just wishful thinking. So instead I came up with the idea for this book, especially "The Boomerang Book" part of it. In hopes to be an inspiration to the many out there like myself, who will care enough to be the keeper of the "gems" (as I like to call them) And by giving this book to one of your own loved ones; be it your mother, father, grandparent, aunt, uncle, etc. They will finally have a place to write their very own stories, maybe even put a few pictures in it; or perhaps a favorite recipe! Remind them during your presentation of your hopes that these gems (the good the bad and the funny) one day will be returned to you, never to be lost…but to be cherished forevermore. Because you are not only someone who happens to loves this person, you will truly be delighted in reading and sharing their stories with others as well. And who knows, you might have a future Novel there, or even possibly…a Lifetime Movie!

Also, if I may suggest; give them what I use to call, a "lucky pen" to go with their workbook, scrapbook, journal…whatever you choose to call it (And yes, I do have a lucky pen story to tell and I'll be putting it in my own Boomerang Book; and trust me, lucky pens work…just ask my kids!) Then perhaps ask your loved one to put the book on a coffee table, bedside table, or someplace where they can easily see it; so when they do think of a story (be it their own or even a family story) they'll be able to quickly jot it down. Because, no one should die with their stories in them…they need to write them down.

The Boomerang Book

Dear _____

    You mean so much to me, I wanted to give you a place to write all your wonderful stories; some I remember and some I don't, but I want to be able to remember every single one of them. So one day, when it is full of your delightful stories, I'd like it back…because I love you!

Sincerely, _____

My name is_____

I was born on this date_____

I was born in_____

My parent's names were_____

The following pages are filled with stories I love to tell…I truly hope you enjoy reading them!

Story #1

Story #2

Story #3

Story #4

Story #5

Story #6

Story #7

Story #8

Story #9

Story #10

Story #11

Story #12

Story #13

Story #14

Story #15

Story #16

Story #17

Story #18

Story #19

Story #20

Story #21

Story #22

Story #23

Story #24

Story #25

Story #26

Story #27

Story #28

Story #29

Story #30

Story #31

Story #32

Story #33

Story #34

Story #35

Story #36

Story #37

Story #38

Story #39

Story #40

Story #41

Story #42

Story #43

Story #44

Story #45

Story #46

Story #47

Story #48

Story #49

Story #50

Back at ya!

I _____ hereby request, when I am no longer around

to tell my stories, this Book will become the property of_____

Thank you for caring enough to ask! Sincerely, _____

My letter to the Giver

Acknowledgements

To my Brother Pat and my Sister Leanne: thank you for helping me to remember some of our mom's wonderful stories…we are the keepers of the gems!

To my youngest son Landon: thank you for that awesome road trip and reminding me that my stories are important too!

To my oldest son Bronson: Thank you for your support in helping me with the artwork parts of my books…you are such a talent!

Visit http://bronsonharley.com to see more of my son's beautiful works of ART

Check out my Novel "I Thought She'd Be Prettier" by Diana Lee on Amazon.com

Also join Facebook https://www.facebook.com/StoriesMyMotherNeverToldMe

And a special thank you to those who purchased this book. One day you'll appreciate the little gems it will hold…God bless you for caring enough <3

Random Thoughts!

Random Thoughts!

Random Thoughts!

CPSIA information can be obtained
at www.ICGtesting.com
Printed in the USA
LVOW04s1355020517
532992LV00012B/124/P

9 781545 125908